F*CK YES
MANIFEST

THE ULTIMATE SIDEKICK
FOR YOUR SIDE HUSTLE

LAUREN ANDREWS

First Published in the United States of America in 2020.

Paperback ISBN: 978-1-7360264-0-3

TABLE OF CONTENTS

PART 1: FIGURE OUT YOUR F*CK

PART 2: MANIFEST THAT SH!T

"Those who use foul language... are sending an expensive signal that they are free - and, ironically, competent. You don't signal competence if you don't take risks for it - there are few such low-risk strategies. So cursing today is a status symbol, just as oligarchs in Moscow wear blue jeans at special events to signal their power."
- Nassim Taleb, Skin In The Game

This book is for the business baddies, the boujee butterflies, the Unicorn Exchange gang, and all the future unicorns to come. My hope is that the challenges and stories in this book help you claim the power, freedom, and status you have been denied. That you not simply say "Yes" - but a bold, vivacious "F*ck Yes" to everything you want to experience in this life.

Everything is possible.

My undying gratitude to those that make my life so much sweeter: Hannah, Kieran, Abby, Yelena, Staci, Linh, Nikki, and my Frank. Love you all always.

RESOURCES

To make sure you get the most out of saying F*ck Yes to your goals, we've put together a few resources to set you up for success. Enjoy!

Free F*ck Yes Workbook & Email Challenge
unicornexchange.com/fyes-workbook
Get each day's challenge straight to your inbox along with the worksheets for each challenge.

F*ck Yes Framework Video Course
unicornexchange.com/fyes
Want an extra layer of inspiration? Get the entire framework on video to listen to, plus bonus interviews and resources to support your goals.

Free Online Community For Womxn
unicornexchange.com/join
To make the most out of the work you're going to put in while going through the challenges of this book, make sure you join our community & get connected.

Keep The Magic Alive 90 Day Planner
unicornexchange.com/90
Once you complete this framework, we've created a bundle to help you keep the magic going. Visit the url above to get your 90 planner + bonus gifts. Use the code: yesunicorn for 10% off.

HELLO UNICORN

If you're reading this I believe you have something big coming your way. In your mind you have a new vision stirring. You're ready to get started in making it a reality.

Easier said than done. Not only is it difficult to start taking action on a new dream, it's even harder when you don't have the clarity on what your actual goal is... or purpose... or message...

That's where this book comes to play. This is your ultimate sidekick for turning your vision into action.

- In Part 1 you'll encounter a series of challenges designed to help you clarify your path forward.
- Part 2 is all about making it happen, with a 4 week planner to help you get your mission in motion.

To further support your journey and help you along your way, join our online community at unicornexchange.com/join

My hope is that as you go through this framework, you unapologetically say F*CK YES to your deepest dreams and highest self. The world needs more magic. I'm so grateful that you're chosen to share your YES with us.

Everything is Possible,

Lauren

PART 1

FIGURE OUT YOUR F*CK

1

PLAY
BIGGER

If you're familiar with the Unicorn Exchange, then you know we focus on empowering womxn in business. Rest assured, even if you don't fit that mold, you are welcome and you are in the right place.

No matter who you are, if you're trying to play bigger in life, you're in the right place. If you feel a mix between butterflies and restlessness and pure excitement when you think about all you want to create and experience in this life, again, you are in the right place.

Before we dive in too deep, I want to make sure we're on the same page. The ultimate purpose of this framework is to unapologetically nurture your ambitions and to relentlessly support your goals.

While equal rights have come a long way in the last 100 years, there is still so much to be done; especially when it comes to breaking the social constructs that have been mindlessly taught and passed down from generation to generation; especially, when it comes to women playing small.

The damage is as real as ever.

The perfect example came to light because of this manifest. When I first envisioned what is now this workbook, I wanted to kick off the concept as an event, which of course I was gung-ho in naming none other than "Fuck Yes Fest".

Throughout the design of the event, I was very mindful of every detail *especially the name*. It became very intentional. I wanted to create a polarization in order to attract a very specific audience.

Obviously "fuck" is an offensive word to many.
I was convinced the name would be the perfect filter and magnet for the right attendees. Ultimately, I was right.

The event successfully attracted those who approach life with curiosity. Those spiritual gangsters that believe in magic, but also know when to hustle; the unicorns that want to live a thousand lives in one and experience every ounce of possibility the universe has for them.

In an almost ironic fashion I said, "Fuck It" and went full force with the name, knowing I would have to be very precise in the advertisement targeting and that regardless there would be at least a minor degree of backlash. Honestly, I was gratefully surprised at the lack of backlash. The worst comment received was "Is this a sex thing?" ... Which I mean, 1) Isn't bad and 2) I should have seen it coming.

It was 2 days before the event, when it finally happened. Cue the pitchfork and torch.

No, There wasn't an angry mob. Just an angry... mom.

Turns out she didn't even see the advertisement for the event, but rather a post on social media. One I didn't even write. With the sacred "F" word.

There are few times that I could even start to describe my mom as angry. Boy, oh boy. Now was one of those times. She was livid and she let me know it.

I was crushed by the glance of a single text. Every ounce of excitement over what I had created left my body and in its place gut wrenching anxlety.

"Why would she choose to focus on a single word and not the heart of the mission? Did she not know she was throwing me a curveball at the worst time? How malicious."

After a night of sulking, I woke to the realization that this was exactly why I was working so hard on this event. This was the reason I started exploring this framework in the first place.

THIS.

This cultural norm that daughters have blindly inherited from their mothers.

This notion that sticking to the 'proper lady' script is more important than speaking freely. The idea that the way you say something is more important than what you say. That showing face is more important than speaking the truth. That above all, we must behave.

Any deviation from this script means we must work even harder for our voices to be heard.

The purpose of this manifesting framework is to give you another tool in your arsenal to fight this small syndrome.

The Small Syndrome, to be a woman is to shrink.

This narrative has been written over and over again throughout history. As much as the cycle has been interrupted, it's only through a filter. With each generation a little more suppression is taken away. The stain fads with each cycle, but it's still there.

We still have a way to go.

We have to be mindful in this fight.
Mindful in saying yes to taking up space.
Mindful in being unapologetic for the life you want.
Mindful in speaking up even when they try to drown
your voice.
Mindful in saying not just yes, but FUCK YES! to your
goals.

This manifest is so much more than a weird book/journal
love child.

It is a space for you to be unapologetically yourself and
breathe life into your next vision. Because I know that
the world needs your dreams to become a reality. There
is someone, many someones, that need you to live your
best life, so they can live theirs.

If you're having trouble committing to your new project,
remember those that you're serving. What hope are you
giving them? How are you helping make their life better?

If you don't follow through with your dream, you are
hindering someone from fulfilling theirs. No it's not going
to stop them completely, but it will slow them down.

This manifest is designed with the intent of making your
most audacious goals a reality.

I firmly believe that a largely discounted reason women often feel a "lack of vision" and even burnout, is that they don't have the encouragement they need to get through bouts of discouragement.

When you start to chase audacious dreams, if you begin with a lack of encouragement and then you face additional discouragement, you're now operating with a deficit. Your internal cheerleader count goes into the negative.

It's no wonder those unsolicited messages that tell you not to do it your way leave a negative impact. When you start with an ounce of self doubt, those additional drops tend to add up fast.

Let's get a better picture of the battle we're facing here. This Small Syndrome is ingrained into western culture. I highly recommend reading Mary Beard's essay on history, "Women & Power: A Manifesto". Her book brings to light the dynamic of male vs female power in Homer's Odyssey.

Yes, The Odyssey. The foundation of Western literature. The beginning of Western record. Ancient notes on how women were treated in past civilizations. Beard mentions that Telemachus is taught that "A significant part of growing up is learning to take control of public speech."

She cites an example of this in how he silences his mother - the woman who pushed him out of the birth canal - for simply suggesting a change to the music. Not only does he tell his mom to shut up, but then he sends her to her quarters to get back to work at the loom. "Boooo Telemachus" - Me.

This hierarchy of vocal authority has evolved.

Yet, we've continued to teach our daughters that to be a good woman is to be quiet. To not say 'Fuck yes' to our ambitions and our own unique voice. Here's the thing though, it's no use to blame our mothers or grandmothers. They were only taught the same.

Here's the catch. We're no longer ignorant to this cycle. You and me, we see what's going on here. Ignoring it will not only harm ourselves, but the womxn to come after us. As I mentioned before, you not using your voice isn't going to prevent your niece or daughter from using hers. But, it's not going to help. We must break these patterns in ourselves. Not only for our own sake but for future generations of women...

That's what we're here to do; break the pattern of playing small.

Are you ready to give yourself space to focus on your goals and aspirations?

I'll say it one more time. This manifest is all about unapologetically nurturing your ambitions and relentlessly supporting your goals.

Okay, enough with the battle cry. If you've made it this far, then you're in the right place and it's time to kick the Small Syndrome's ass. It's time to face your first challenge.

You know the saying sometimes it has to get worse before it gets better? … Well it's not going to get worse here, but it is going to get messier before we tidy up and get those thoughts organized.

The challenge is to write out your download. What is your vision? How are you going to be playing bolder in life? What are you saying fuck yes to during this journey?

On the next page, you'll find an area to do a massive brain dump.

I like braindumps, better than brainstorms. Brainstorms imply coming up with new ideas.

Braindumps are all about emptying the genius ideas that have been floating around in your mind palace.

WHAT'S YOUR DOWNLOAD?

First things first, write down everything that has been circulating in your mind about this new vision. Put a timer on for 2 minutes, take a deep breath and press start. Now, without erasing anything, write out everything that you want to manifest. What revelations and new ideas have come to mind? Anything goes.
Write out everything you've received.

Once you're done, post a photo in the group! Find synchronicities & let the universe conspire in your favor.
Facebook.com/groups/unicornexchangeco

2

VISION
AUDIT

Time to start decoding your download. The goal of this chapter is to audit your current actions and make sure you're on the right track for making your goal a reality.

Think of it as opening up your GPS and pressing the find location button. But instead of your position on earth, you're able to see how close you are to making your dream a reality.

If you had the chance to gauge how close you are to your dream destination and if you're on the most efficient route to get there, would you take it?

Sometimes our Goal Positioning System (see what I did there) gets out of calibration.

We're humans so we're pretty susceptible to "shiny object syndrome." If there is the chance to stop at Laverne's Pie Shop, we're going to take it. Anything to make the ride sweeter. Too many detours, though, and we can forget why we're on the road in the first place. Shit happens.

When you realize you're somewhere you don't want to be, you have to first figure out where the hell you are.

When it comes to your ambitions and your everyday life, what are you working on? Do you have a full time 9-5 job while exploring creating passive income with a new blog? Are you entrenched in your business, but you've started dabbling with a new side product?

A question to consider: what has made your to-do list this last week? Where has your energy gone? To figure out where you are, we need to know how you're devoting your time.

Once you understand the full scope of what you're devoting your time to, you're able to find gaps where you can devote time to this new idea.

At the end of this chapter you're going to find an exercise called the "Vision Venn Diagram". I ask you to write out everything that's hitting your to-do list and compare it with what you need to do, to make this vision a real thing.

Throughout this exercise, it's important to write out everything that comes to mind and it is so important to write unfiltered to help find the incongruences and synchronicities between what you *are* doing and what you *want* to be doing.

For all exercises in this manifest, I recommend setting a timer for each question. At least 2 minutes. This provides a container to meditate on each question and helps reduce the need to rush.

A few thoughts to guide you through this challenge:

- When you check out this challenge you'll find a circle label "The Now". Focus on the present and jot down every project that you're currently working on. What items have been making your to do list? Any project in your business, any hobbies, work responsibilities, even home life responsibilities can make the list.

- Once your allotted time is up, it's time to move over to "The Dream" circle. Here you'll host a conscious stream of journaling about every hope and dream that you want to accomplish: a shift from focusing on what you're doing now, to what you want *now*.

- Some of these goals might be short term, others might be 50 years away. Anything and everything goes. As you're writing these out, think about your desires that you want so badly that you tend to guard them. You know those goals that you're shy to talk about because if you put it out there it feels like you're risking something. Those dreams that risk the perception of being unrealistic or stupid. Those are the dreams I'm talking about. Now is not the time to be timid in your hopes. Be unapologetic. Be bold. Write down your deepest desires and hopes. You should feel a little resistance, this is normal. You should be tapping into your deepest desires that you have a natural tendency to guard and keep safe.

After both circles are complete, it's time to get into audit mode. In the center of the diagram sits the common ground between your current reality and *what could be*. Sounds mystical?

Well, it kind of is. This is your chance to figure out what magic is already at work or what you need to create in order for The Now to transform into The Dream.

A few questions to consider:

- What does The Now have in common with The Dream? What attributes stay the same? Focus on cultivating these projects!

- If there isn't much in the middle, what can you add to The Now, to gain commonality with The Dream?

- Maybe there isn't a direct correlation, and maybe you need a stepping stone in the middle: something to bridge what you're doing now to what you want to be doing. This could be finding a new gig, or a new hire; an initiative to bring a part of The Dream over to the Now.

- You might need space to come back to this. Depending on how meditative you get, you might need to take a break.

- To wrap up this challenge, what are you committed to in the next 90 days?

Pick one project from the common ground: something in the works you can expand off of, or something that you need to create to start building your bridge.

What Common Ground Initiative are you going to say Fuck Yes to over the next 90 days?

UNICORN FOR
YOUR THOUGHTS?

USE THIS BLANK PAGE TO CAPTURE
YOUR THOUGHTS, WRITE NOTES, OR
CREATE A LITTLE DOODLE

YOUR VISION
VENN DIAGRAM

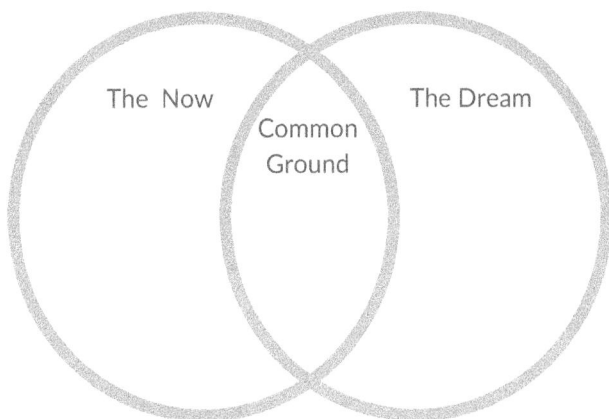

The Now   Common   The Dream
           Ground

1. **The Now:** List out every project you are currently working on. Anything that has been making your to-do list, or you know should be, counts!

2. **The Dream:** Take your download from Challenge 1 & organize your thoughts into bite sized projects. Group like ideas that you could accomplish in about 90 days.

3. **The Common Ground:** Take a look at all the projects on both the left and right side of the diagram. Write down all points of commonality. What can you add to the middle of the diagram to start transitioning what you're working on now to suite your dreams.

4. **Circle Your Focus.** Choose 1 item listed in the Common Ground to commit to working on for the next 90 days. Get your favorite pen out and circle it!

3

HOLDING BACK

It's time to tackle the Small Syndrome. This challenge is all about facing the Small Syndrome head on.

It's a check-up for your ambition. In the previous challenge, we checked in on your journey to making your vision a reality. Now, we're making sure your ambition is healthy enough to make the journey.

This isn't going to be another project you start and put to the side after a couple of days. We're seeing this through to the end.

For this thing to last, you have to make sure your ambition is healthy; that you have the energy and confidence needed to manifest this shit.

What is the number one factor in an unhealthy ambition? An out of control case of the Small Syndrome. The Small Syndrome is what I call the social disease that continues to tell women to shrink. It's ingrained in most social hierarchies, western civilization included. I mentioned earlier that there are even Homeric references of this paradigm. Generations of social constructs that tell us that women should be quieter, softer, kinder, less assertive and while you're at it make sure you shrink a couple of dress sizes, too. When you internalize all that bullshit, it becomes the Small Syndrome.

Here's the sucky part: I don't believe there is an antidote to this. It is a chronic disease.

An antidote is instant, but this parasitic mindset has to be fought continually. We can't just wipe it out and be done with it, because unfortunately we were born into it.

But, with a healthy regime for your confidence, you can keep your ambition in good health. If you consume the right things to nourish your soul, you can have the drive you need to accomplish these big goals.

To maintain overall good health, you must dedicate the time and attention it takes to treat all the different aspects of your health. The same goes for your goals: they have to be treated holistically.

Your mind, your body, and your spirit all play into not letting this sickness, this small syndrome, pull you from your goal.

In this challenge there are a couple of questions I'd like you to consider.
- What are your symptoms of the small syndrome?
- What ambition ailments are showing in your day to day?
- What is giving you anxiety?
- When it comes time to work on your goal, what excuses tend to come up?

When I first addressed these questions, my primary symptom was when it comes to my business, no one can do it like me: nobody really values my business and products like I do. I can't trust someone to do the job like I can. I just can't find enough good help.

It's likely that your symptoms show up differently. You might feel that you don't think anyone wants to hear your voice. Maybe you're just always too busy. You need to fix XYZ before you can get started. What shows up for you?

What do you call your syndrome?

After writing down your symptoms and having them laid out in front of you.

Let's take a step back and get real on how you refer to these symptoms.

Read through the symptoms you've listed.

When you read through these symptoms what label do you put on yourself?

What have you accepted as true or as being "just" you?

It's "just" your personality.

For me, I'm just a control freak; that's why I can't enroll people in my vision.

That's why I have to do everything myself. If my name is on it, it has to be perfect. I am just a control freak. Yikes.

That was how the small syndrome was showing up in my life.

This could also be something that others - family, friends, a loved one has labeled you.

You might even find this label endearing.

Other common names.... *I'm just a procrastinator, I'm just not smart enough, I'm not experienced, I don't have the credentials, I am too busy.*

What will you add to your regimen?

Like I said, there isn't an antidote.

But there is still a path to health via regimen.

When I realized that I was hiding under the guise of being a control freak, the solution was crystal clear. I needed to hire more help. I did it within an hour. I couldn't unsee it and I didn't want to hold myself back any longer.

What is one actionable step you can take to fight the Small Syndrome and start alleviating the symptoms that are currently holding you back?

It could be finding a therapist or waking up an hour earlier for "you time." Maybe it means finding a mastermind for support or exploring audio books to expand your expertise. What will you add to your regime to support a healthy ambition?

After you complete the questions at the end of chapter, I'm going to ask you to take this a step further.

The real challenge of this chapter is exercising vulnerability. I'm going to ask that once you complete this challenge, you take a picture of your worksheet and send it to someone. It can be your partner or friend.

You can even message it to @UnicornExchangeCo on social! Just someone, anyone! Sharing how you're holding back is the most important thing you can do for overcoming these rough patches.

The thing about vulnerability is that it is the antidote for loneliness. There isn't an antidote for the Small Syndrome, but there is for loneliness.

And loneliness is a bitch. A bitch that creates the perfect environment for other nasty ailments, like the Small Syndrome, to thrive. Whenever my boyfriend and I started dating I was dealing with trying to solve a clusterfuck of a tax issue.

I had recently found out that a past accountant never sent in my filings and while I originally owed very little that year I had ended up accruing thousands of dollars in penalties and having to refile and so on and so forth. I was so embarrassed by the situation, that I had let something so simple get past me. (Remember the whole "I'm a control freak" thing, I took pride in that).

I did not want him to know about this.

We had been friends for 6 years before we started dating. We knew each other really well and both looked at each other as successful business owners. I did not want him to think I was a fraud. I was so embarrassed that I somehow let this mistake happen and I didn't want him to know.

Thankfully, when I fessed up to what was bothering me, he was able to share how he had dealt with a similar situation and how a close, crazy successful, friend of ours had experienced the same thing but 10x the severity... and everything ended up fine.

In an instant the panic and loneliness dispersed. Everything was going to be okay with my business, he still loved me, and I had recommendations to remedy the situation.

I had better solutions than I could have come up with on my own.

When you exercise vulnerability, with the right people, you're creating space for the universe to give you the answers you wouldn't have considered otherwise. So please, share your answers to this challenge with someone. You might just find a better solution to the struggles you're battling.

UNICORN FOR
YOUR THOUGHTS?
USE THIS BLANK PAGE TO CAPTURE
YOUR THOUGHTS, WRITE NOTES, OR
CREATE A LITTLE DOODLE.

WHAT'S HOLDING YOU BACK

For each question below set a timer for 2 minutes. Meditate on each question & write down your answers unedited. Allow your thoughts to flow authentically.

What are your symptoms?

What do you call this sickness?

What will you add to your regimine?

The real challenge of today! Share what has been holding you back with someone. Text your revelation to your accountability buddy, send us an email, or snap a photo and post in the Facebook group! Embracing vulnerability, finding out you're not alone is the best thing you can do for your ambition.

4

MESSAGE CLARITY

How do you craft a brand so compelling that it breaks through belief systems? It's time to turn up the volume on your message so that you are heard. You have this amazing new vision and it's time to enroll others! How do you make sure that you are doing your mission justice and making sure it's not lost in the crowd of advertising?

I once heard a speaker open their presentation with a statistic that in 2009 it took a buyer 5 reference points to make a buying decision. Then, by 2016 that number shot up to 29. What used to take 5 marketing points, now needs six times the exposure to enroll a customer. In full disclosure, I've tried finding this statistic and I've had no luck finding its source.

I'd imagine this number changes with how saturated a particular market is as well. Regardless, it gives a shining example as to how technology has impacted advertising. It speaks to why you're followed by curated ads everywhere you go.

The advertising floodgates have been opened. If your messaging isn't clear your voice is going to be drowned out. There are two paths to getting visibility: volume and deviance. If you have the budget, you have the ability to be seen everywhere. Think about legacy brands like Coca-Cola.

Everyone knows what Coke is; it's recognized worldwide, yet they still advertise. Once you're known, you still have to continue to be relevant. More than relevant: omnipresent. Even if you're not a soft drink type of person, you are still aware of new flavors or campaigns they're dropping. This omnipresence means their message has infiltrated the belief systems of millions of people.

They take up real estate in the minds of consumers across the world. They're able to do this with a massive advertising budget, but it didn't start off that way; they had to take the alternative route of deviance first. They had to be different. Coca-Cola was invented and started its journey to fame by becoming a temperance drink during prohibition.

Not only was it a non-alcoholic drink, but it was created by a pharmacist with the intent of being great for your health.

It was a standout product in its time. Of course, we all know now that its health claims weren't necessarily correct and that the coca plant certainly helped with its success.

If you're like most who are starting off on a new venture, it's best to go the route of deviance. How can your message deviate from others in your niche? How do you make sure you're not adding to the noise of marketing and that your message isn't just standing out, but actually understood and received.

The best type of deviance comes from understanding your audience and teaching them how you can help them. It starts with taking your audience down the road of digestible education.

You would never give a kindergartener an SAT test and expect them to pass. That's ludicrous. Expecting someone unfamiliar with your brand to buy into your message is the same. Kinda ridiculous.

We all go through a system of education when it comes to what we buy, if we're aware of it or not. This can come in the form of seeking out reviews or casually checking out an article that shows up in our newsfeed.

Every human is becoming more aware of how marketing works. You might even find that your technologically challenged grandparents are making comments about how they were talking about new shoes and got an ad for the exact pair they were interested in on Facebook.

With so much noise floating around the internet and advertising being more accessible than ever, not only do you have to continually try and stand out but you also have to earn the trust of your potential audience.

Remember you're a part of someone's audience, too. I bet that 3 years ago you were a lot more likely to buy something just seeing it once than you are today.

As a consumer it is important to feel safe and to trust a brand. So how do you build that trust? How do you meet someone where they are, to educate them to the point of becoming a trusting buyer.

It comes down to education. Nurturing your audience with the building blocks they need to receive and understand the information you're giving out.

For this challenge, we're taking advice from my favorite messaging magician, Yelena Reese*. In her Persuasion Playbook she explains how to take someone from the

*Learn more about Yelena at yelenareese.com

first point of contact to the point of influence. The point of influence being, the exact moment where your potential customer transforms into an actual customer. The point where an individual has been educated enough that you have earn enough of their trust for them to make a buying decision with you.

Much of what we're touching on in this challenge is a part of her Belief Sequence roadmap.

Now, you are going to complete your own messaging map. Throughout this exercise we are going to be referencing your Unicorn, your dream customer.

The goal is to be able to give this trusty steed your messaging map with the goal that they'll find their way to the end of the map: you!

Before you turn to your worksheet, here are a few questions to consider.

1. Who is your Unicorn and where are they starting?

What is their problem?

This is a bit more than just identifying an avatar. What are the questions and thoughts that your Unicorn is asking to put them in a spot of being receptive to education in your area of expertise?

2. What is the destination? We're skipping ahead to the end of the map for this one.

> What is your desired outcome from your message?

> Where do we want your Unicorn to end up? We're starting with the end in sight.

> What is the final point of education that your customer needs to be able to trust you? This could look like making a specific purchase, opting in to a lead magnet, hopping on a sales call.

> What is the ultimate end goal you want to achieve through your message?

Now to fill in the middle of this map.

3. What is your customer's sign that you're the one?

> What does your Unicorn need to understand and learn *right* before saying "yes" to you? Before they take the final exit to arrive at their destination, they need a sign that clearly denotes where to turn off.

> What is your audience asking right before they decide your offer is the best solution to their problem? They are likely asking, "what is a solution?" before trusting that your solution is the best choice.

If you're a realtor, before a seller chooses to list with YOU, they need to know that listing with a realtor will get them the best price.

They have to understand that a realtor is the solution before they understand that YOU are the best realtor for that solution. If you are a health and wellness coach, the audience needs to understand why they first need a coach before they choose you.

One more stop to complete our messaging map.

4. What's your Unicorn's fuel stop?

Once they're given the map, they need energy to make it to the exit sign and ultimately the final destination. What does your Unicorn need to know in order to make it through the rest of the journey?

What encouragement, hope, or shiny object do you need to give your audience so they continue their path of education with you?

Back to the realtor example, before they decide to list with you, before they decide the need to sell their house with a realtor, they need to know it's a sellers market. That now is the best time to list. They need the ounce of encouragement that now is the opportune time to go on this journey.

Now that you've gone through these questions it's time for you to complete your messaging map in the correct order of the Unicorn's journey. This messaging map is a great reference point for educating your audience. By delivering each of these stops as a different piece of content you're guiding your audience to understand why you're the best choice to solve their problem and to ultimately choose you.

MESSAGING MAP

For each question below set a timer for 2 minutes.
Meditate on each question & write down your answers
unedited. Allow your thoughts to flow authentically.

Who is your Unicorn & where are they starting?

What does your Unicorn need to take off?
What do they need to continue following your map?

What's your Unicorn's Exit Sign? Now that your Unicorn
is engaged in this journey with you, what do they need to
know right before they reach their destination?

What is your desired outcome from your message?
What ultimate action you want your unicorn to take?

5

BE A
HELPER

A quick note before we dive into this challenge. I want to express my gratitude for your involvement in this framework. Here is the bigger picture: you choosing to play bigger and actually take the time out of your day to focus on manifesting your gifts and talents is world-changing important.

Mindfully choosing to shake up your routine results in new perspectives and possibilities.

The world needs you.

Rachel D Fox* gives a killer presentation on imposter syndrome, I was lucky enough to have her as a presenter for F*ck Yes Fest 2020. In her keynote she gave the perfect example for why your individual message is needed. She tells a story about how she has taught all 11

*Learn more about Rachel at racheldfox.com

her kids (yes, 11) the simple, well known fact that 1+1=2. As hard as she tried to teach them this, they didn't understand until they went to school and learned from each of their teachers that 1+1 does, in fact, equal 2. It didn't click for them until they were taught by their unique, specific teachers. Rachel then explains that you are someone's unique, specific teacher.

Your message, your product, no matter how unoriginal you think it is-- is needed. It is unique. Even if you don't see it. There are people out there who speak the same language your soul speaks and they need your voice.

Which brings me to this chapter's topic. Advocacy!

Not only are there those that can easily receive your voice, but there are those that need you to use your voice on their behalf.

If you're reading this, I have no doubt that you have the makings of a world changer. You live your life in a way that consistently helps those around you. If you're here, now, you also believe that business is about more than just profits. It's about people, too.

Slowly, society has been transitioning to a consumer aware market. It seems like with the break of 2020, we've hit a new peak of conscious consumerism. Overnight, social justice seems to have become a branch of every major corporation's marketing team. Almost in an unnerving way.

The goal of this chapter isn't to make advocacy trendy. Injustice shouldn't ever be a marketing ploy. Using the gifts and reach that your organization curates is bad ass though.

It might seem like a fine line, but as long as your actions speak louder than your words, you can't go wrong. While being vocal about your support and values is great, actions are key. So that's what we're looking at in this chapter.

What actions can you take to be the ultimate helper?

When you receive a new vision, there is usually some greater good to it. Unfortunately, when projects develop, that cause can be lost rather quickly. However, if you start out with laser clarity on what you're advocating for, it can be ingrained in the culture from the start. If this is you, this is truly a "putting your money where your mouth is" type of challenge.

Or perhaps, you have fallen into a rut, where you want to be a top notch advocate, but you're waiting for the stars to align or to reach a certain revenue. Whatever the reason, you just haven't implemented any initiatives yet. Now is time and place to plan it out.

For this challenge you're going to walk through a series of questions....

1. What are you advocating for?

This might sound simple, but try and make this as specific as possible.

- If you are to choose one thing to fight for the rest of your life what would it be?
- What is your big social cause?
- What brings out the social justice warrior in you.
- What's worth fighting for to you?

2. How does this currently show up in your business?

Read through all the questions below to really open your mind to all the actions you're taking to be an advocate, that you might not even realize.

- Is this cause something you talk about publicly in your business? How about with your team?
- Do you create content about it?
- Do you have initiatives to support your cause?
- Do you regularly donate?
- Are there mentorship opportunities that support this cause?

If there isn't anything, that's okay. We're going to dive

into what you can create in the next question.

3. What is one new way to add to your advocacy game, that you haven't already been implementing?

- If you're not doing anything, what can you start?
- If you have a few initiatives going already then what can you add?

Now is the time to get creative. If you feel like you're lacking the creative juices on this question, I really suggest reaching out to other Unicorns in our free Facebook community.

Many in this group have gone through this process and you'd be amazed at the creativity that has come out of these collaborations. Mentorship programs, scholarships, creative donation campaigns, the list goes on.

There are amazing conversations that have been spurred because of this topic and I know that if you were to engage it will spark new ideas for your use as well.

Now that your wheels are turning, it's time to write out your thoughts. Turn to your Implementing Advocacy exercise and write out your answers to these questions.

Then you'll compile these reflections into an advocacy statement for your vision.

Once you have completed the questions on the next page, flip over and complete your advocacy statement. Once it's complete, it should sound something like this....

> *I, Lauren, have chosen to use my business as a tool for social change. I am committing to use the resources that Unicorn Exchange generates to advocate for women's rights. I am stepping up my advocacy game by implementing the following into my business operations: mentorship opportunities and quarterly donations for STEM education for girls.*

At Unicorn Exchange we are all about using our businesses for the forces of good.

If you haven't joined our free Facebook group yet, hop on over and share your advocacy statement.
You can join at unicornexchange.com/join

I'm looking forward to seeing what cause you're passionate about!

IMPLEMENTING ADVOCACY

What are you advocating for?

How does this currently show up in your business?

What is one new way to add to your advocacy game that you haven't been implementing?

ADVOCACY STATEMENT

I, ..., have chosen to use my business as a tool
_(name)

for social change. I am committing to use the resources

that .... generates to advocate for I
_{business/project name} _(cause)

am stepping up my advocacy game by implementing the

following into my business operations:

....

....

....

Signed: ....

Date: ....

6

GET OUT THERE

If you've made it to this point, pop a bottle. You kept your commitment to yourself and continued to show up for your vision.

I really want you to pause, take a moment, and think about what you've done for yourself, your business, and subsequently those that you impact.

It's big.

You chose to give your time and energy to creating something good in the world.

You repeatedly set aside time for your hopes, your dreams, and your vision.

You prioritized the change you wish to bring in the world. That's huge. You didn't have to fly across the country to attend a conference to produce life changing energy. You were able to do that right from home. You had it in you all along. The vision just needed a bit of attention, to be nurtured and cared for. You did that.

In return, you've received a new perspective, and a new invigoration for your goals and life. Now it's time for the cherry on top.

By completing these 5 challenges you now know ...

1. Your vision, what this download the universe has given you really means.

2. What project you need to take on for the next 90 days to make your dream a reality.

3. How you are getting in your way and how you might sabotage yourself: you know what to look out for.

4. How to crank up the volume on your voice and make your message influential.

5. How to amp up your advocacy so that your vision is the ultimate helper.

You did that. That's badass.

Time to share your bad-assery with the world. You've done all this work in nurturing your new vision, friend. You have invested energy and time to understand clearly what this vision needs to be. Now you have to get it out there. I'm not talking about needing a full on product launch. You need to talk about it.

Give it life by starting to socialize it. I know, I'm talking like it's a living breathing animal. Well, it kind of is. If you keep it locked up and just to yourself you're never going to see this thing through. It's going to turn into a fantasy and eventually die. Your dreams take root when they begin to mingle with other ideas, and when they get the feedback and help from others.

Just like any plant, your dream needs soil to take root and grow. Similar to a living being, it needs others to survive. Your vision needs other ideas to grow. It comes in the form of feedback, collaboration, team members creating on your behalf, and customers opting in and purchasing. These are all forms of ideas integrating and mingling with your vision and they are all necessary for it's longevity.

Straight from Psychology Today, "Researchers have found that loneliness is just as lethal as smoking 15 cigarettes per day. Lonely people are 50 percent more likely to die prematurely than those with healthy social relationships."

Maybe you as an individual aren't particularly lonely. But is your business? Is your goal? Are you trying to do it all by yourself? Are you unintentionally keeping your vision and hopes to yourself?

If lonely individuals are 50% more susceptible to premature death, why wouldn't an idea or business? You can control this. Find community, find accountability, and find the relentless support that works for you.

What you are going to share with the world is important.

Who you're going to share it with is vital.

When is of the essence.

At the end of this chapter you'll find these questions waiting for you. You need to answer these and commit to taking action on a daily basis to see your vision come to life. You've spent so much time over the last few chapters actually nurturing your goal. It would be a shame to stop now. Don't do yourself that disservice. This dream will not come to life until you share it with someone.
There's only one thing left:

Committing to seeing this vision through. Continue to nurture it. It's time to sign the papers! Literally. The final challenge is signing a commitment to yourself.

At the end of this chapter you'll find your F*ck Yes Declaration. This is for you to complete and choose to say yes to yourself and choose to play bigger than ever before.

Let's not let your dreams be lonely. Getting support is key for thriving. Let's take that first step and share your answers for the F*ck Yes Commitment with the group. On your declaration you'll find a URL that will direct you to the group.

Complete your F*ck Yes Declaration, sign it, snap a photo, and share.

You're starting a new project and you need all the support you can get. Why not start here and find out who is ready to join you and help?

I'm full of gratitude that you went through this entire framework with me. That you stepped up to the plate and took on the challenge of playing bigger.

Don't worry, there is plenty more to come, now it's time to get into the grit of it. It's time to start executing the actions you need to take this vision and turn it into a reality. See you in part 2 for your next 4 week challenge! Let's get to work!

GET IT OUT THERE

You know the drill by now. For each question below set a timer for 2 minutes to complete your response. Meditate on each question and write down your answers unedited. Allow your thoughts to flow authentically.

What are you going to share with the world?

List 3 people you're going to share your vision with.

When are you going to share it by?

Who is your blessing (your unicorn tribe)?

Now it's time to go to the next page and complete your F*ck Yes Declaration! Make sure you post in the Facebook group. This is important. It's time to share your idea with the world and start meeting those that will be crucial in helping you make your vision a reality.

Facebook.com/groups/unicornexchangeco

F*CK YES
DECLARATION

I am committed to turning my ideas into a reality. I will **prioritize my vision** to nurture my dreams and focus on giving them life. I'll act with courage.

I will be mindful of the Small Syndrome and overcome any obstacles thrown my way. Most importantly, I will cherish my health holistically: mind, body, spirit, and ambition.

I'm **ready to be heard** as a leader. I know that dreaming will only take me so far and I am committed to taking action, sharing my vision, and **leaving a legacy** with my work.

I choose to grow from the challenges that will come my way. I choose to live a bold life. I choose to be unapologetic in chasing my goals. I choose to say **F*CK YES to my vision** and play bigger than ever before. I see my strengths and believe everything is possible.

My Vision: ....

Signed: .... **Date:** ....

SO, WHAT'S NEXT?

Not only did you say F*ck Yes to living bolder, playing bigger, and making your dreams turn into reality. You've embodied that vision by showing up and taking action.

You've said, "Thank you Universe for the sign, let's do it!" Now prepare to reap the rewards of your actions & see how the universe shows up. Big things are ahead.

So... What's Next? It's time to get to work!
You've figured out what you give a f*ck about & now it's time to make it happen. Remember, you don't have to do it alone. Even if you're an established Business Owner, starting a new project is always easier with a solid support system. If you don't have a support system, I'd like to invite you to make your unicorn status official. Head over to UnicornExchange.com/join

Time for part 2 of this book-journal love child. This next section is designed to help you organize & keep track of your project. When implementing a new vision, it's often best to hold a separate container so it doesn't get lost in your day-to-day priorities. In the next section of this book, we'll kick off by planning out your next 30 days so that you are clear on your weekly priorities. This way, you know exactly what you need to be working on each day to move this bad boy forward.

Remember, you are magic. Everything is possible.

PART 2

MANIFEST THAT SH!T

SO, HOW IS THIS HALF GOING TO WORK?

Now that you've completed Part 1 of the F*ck Yes Manifest, it's time to put all that planing into action. It's time to put your magic to work and start manifesting.

The second half of this book is all about breaking down those big goals you just created into bite sized actionable pieces that you can check off your to-do list everyday.

What we're really crafting here is a way for you to win everyday. When you start creating a habit of "winning" you're getting a little hit of dopamine each day in relation to your goal. When you mindfully create a positive reaction to something you want, you're setting yourself up for longterm success. You're turning it into a habit.

We're not just getting shit done these next 4 weeks, we're turning your vision into a habit.

If we structure the execution of this project, so that you're creating something you can win at each day, you're creating an addiction like sensation when it comes to working on this vision. Think of it as motivation hacking.

You're planning out your month, week, and day to where you'll be able to check something off your to-do list. The more you win, the longer you're in the game.

So, here is what the next 4 weeks will look like...

Kicking Off With **Monthly Planning**
> Every month you should set aside 30 minutes to focus on what your big vision is. With your big goal in mind, commit to 3 correlating, bite-sized goals to accomplish in the next month, including what key actions are needed to check this off your to-do list.

Staying On Track With **Weekly Intention Setting**
> When a new week comes, it's time to reflect on what you hope to create. Which of your monthly goals and accompanying action items are you committing to?

Moving Forward **Daily Action**
> Before you dive into work for the day, take a moment to acknowledge your wins and get in an affirmation. Remember the goal you're committing to for this week. Then write out which of your action items you'll accomplish. Take time to reflect and then go conquer!

On the next page you'll find an example of how to break down the next 30 days, your week and a day.

If this is your first time adopting a journaling practice, I advise setting a timer *and* creating a calendar event for the entire month. Read more easy tips on how to adopt a successful 'to-do' style journaling practice by visiting unicornexchange.com/journaling-practices

BREAKING DOWN

For each question below set a timer for 2 minutes. Meditate on each question & write down your answers unedited. Allow your thoughts to flow authentically.

What is your big vision?

Increase equality throughout the world by helping womxn live a 'have your cake and eat it too' type of life. Getting more womxn in power and leadership roles, especially in business!

What do you want to have accomplished towards this vision in the next 5 years?

300 active members in the Unicorn Exchange Underground membership, a new brand of physical products for Unicorns growing their businesses launched and grossing over $500k/year, 4 IRL events per year with 90% women on the stage each and every time!

What do you want to have accomplished towards this vision in the next year?

By the end of 2021, we will have 60 referred unicorns in the underground. We will have hosted 3 in person events: 2 UEU only and 1 public. Our podcast will be launched with over 100 episodes.

What are your top 3 goals for the next 4 weeks?
Each goal should take aprx 1 week to complete.

Schedule 23 podcast interviews out for the remainder of this quarter.
Launch fuck yes manifest with 20 "go live and buy" unicorns
Schedule out 2021 UEU events, get feedback on dates.

THE NEXT 4 WEEKS

Below you'll find space to breakdown your 3 goals from the previous page into action items. Keep your timer set for each question. Be mindful in this process.

Goal #1: Schedule 23 podcast interviews out for this quarter

Each action item should take no more than a couple of hours each.

Create sign up form for being a guest on the podcast
Write November newsletter for UEU with sign up linked
Block out time on my calendar for calls 2x a week
Hire a podcast production specialist to edit
Consultation call w/ Marcus Turner about setting up a studio.

Goal #2: Onboard 20 Fuck Yes Manifest ambassadors

Each action item should take no more than a couple of hours each.

Make a list of 20 people that I know I can count on to purchase & review
Reach out these 20 and explain the launch process
Send the ebook version to those that agree to help
Make a calendar invite for the live date & invite the gang

Goal #3: Schedule out 2021 UEU events, get feedback on dates.

Each action item should take no more than a couple of hours each.

Look at my personal calendar and choose preliminary dates
Do any reach outs with the reps for my ideal locations
Reach out to a few UEU girls and see if those work
Post a poll in the group asking for feedback on dates & locations

REFLECTIONS

Think of this as your journey's log. Anything you want to take note of so far? This space is for recording any wins, lessons and ideas for vision expansion.

Below are my actual reflections, it might sound weird and crazy but wanted to give you all a real authentic look at what my F Yes Planning looks like!

WOW... I have been so off lately, my diet is off track and I am feeling it physically and mentally. I need to share this with Frank and we need to do a strict reset this week so I can get back on my game.

I'm thankful for this crazy man. We've gone cold plunging in the river every day this week. Because I thought it was a good idea on Monday and challenged him to go with me, I want to remember though what a difference it makes to get outside and get grounded. Even in crazy bat shit ways. The election is heating up and my brain would have done some massive spiraling if not for this extra hour of outside time and play. It's made a massive difference and I want to remember this for the future.

For the Unicorn Christmas special ...

Let's give away Oragami Unicorn ornaments instructions for every donation. It's digital and a nice little something that will be easy.

Remember to do a project breakdown for the Special so everything goes smooth and nothing is left off the table.... Schedule for the live stream, get linh a list of entertainers, look into other streaming besides zoom, test out live vs prerecorded, get copy done for online giving tree......

Look into the concept of "Permisisonless Leverage"

WEEK 1

I Am Grateful For:
Take a moment to share what you're thankful for.

Living in the middle of no where
My Unicorn Underground girls being a fucking great resource and support
THE HOLIDAYYYYSS ARE HEREEEEE YAAAASSS

My Intention For The Week Is:
What magic do you want to create this week?

Focus on my mental health and how it correlates with the physical.
Pour lots of love and attention into getting the F Yes Manfiest ready for
publish next week ahhhhhhhhhhh

This Week's Goal:
Reference your goals from your 30 day breakdown.

HINT: COPY & PASTE A GOAL FROM THE PREVIOUS PAGE HERE

Onboard 20 Fuck Yes Manifest ambassadors

Action Items To Complete This Week:
Make sure you list the action items from your 30 day breakdown.

COPY & PASTE ACTION ITEMS OF SAID GOAL FROM THE PREVIOUS PAGE HERE

Make a list of 20 people that I know I can count on to purchase & review.
Reach out these 20 and explain the launch process.
Send the ebook version to those that agree to help!
Make a calendar invite for the live date & invite the gang.

"Step out of the history that is holding you back.
Step into the new story you are willing to create."
- Oprah Winfrey

*Use this space to write down any thing on your brain, notes,
more to-dos! Jokes, doodles! This is your blank canvas.*

Remember to put in an order for HEB pick up this afternoon

Send Joel updates for the F Yes Inbox Challenge landing page

Lost mapels reservation for when Nikki is here?

If only I could actually
draw a unicorn this presh.

Today's Date: Monday, November 2nd 2020

My Affirmation:

Everything is possible. I can have my cake and eat it, too.

Wins From Yesterday:

Relaxing Sunday. Didn't open my computer once and barley touched my phone. Got outside and made a lovely dinner with frankie.

This Week's Goal:

THIS IS THE SAME GOAL YOU WROTE ON YOUR WEEKLY PLANNING PAGE. THIS WILL BE THE SAME FOR EVERY DAY THIS WEEK. REPETITION IS KEY.

Onboard 20 Fuck Yes Manifest ambassadors

Today's Action Items:

PICK 1-3 ACTIONS FROM YOUR WEEKLY PLANNING PAGE & LIST THEM HERE.

1. Make a list of 20 people that I know I can count on to purchase & review.
2. Reach out these 20 and explain the launch process if they're interested.
3. Create a spreadsheet to organize all the names & responses

BREAKING DOWN

For each question below set a timer for 2 minutes. Meditate on each question & write down your answers unedited. Allow your thoughts to flow authentically.

What is your big vision?

What do you want to have accomplished towards this vision in the next 5 years?

What do you want to have accomplished towards this vision in the next year?

What are your top 3 goals for the next 4 weeks?
Each goal should take aprx 1 week to complete.

THE NEXT 4 WEEKS

Below you'll find space to breakdown your 3 goals from the previous page into action items. Keep your timer set for each question. Be mindful in this process.

Goal #1:

Each action item should take no more than a couple of hours each.

Goal #2:

Each action item should take no more than a couple of hours each.

Goal #3:

Each action item should take no more than a couple of hours each.

REFLECTIONS

Think of this as your journey's log. Anything you want to take note of so far? This space is great for recording any wins, lessons and ideas for vision expansion.

WEEK 1

I Am Grateful For:
Take a moment to share what you're thankful for.

My Intention For The Week Is:
What magic do you want to create this week?

This Week's Goal:
Reference your goals from your 30 day breakdown.

Action Items To Complete This Week:
Make sure you list the action items from your 30 day breakdown.

"Step out of the history that is holding you back.
Step into the new story you are willing to create."
- Oprah Winfrey

Today's Date:

My Affirmation:

Wins From Yesterday:

This Week's Goal:

Today's Action Items:

"The question isn't who is going to let me; it's who is going to stop me." - Ayn Rand

Today's Date:

My Affirmation:

Wins From Yesterday:

This Week's Goal:

Today's Action Items:

"If you're not making some notable mistakes along the way, you're certainly not taking enough business and career chances." - Sallie Krawcheck

Today's Date:

My Affirmation:

Wins From Yesterday:

This Week's Goal:

Today's Action Items:

"Don't look at your feet to see if you are doing it right. Just dance." - Anne Lamott

Today's Date:

My Affirmation:

Wins From Yesterday:

This Week's Goal:

Today's Action Items:

"And the day came when the risk to remain tight in a bud was more painful than the risk it took to blossom."
- Anaïs Nin

Today's Date:

My Affirmation:

Wins From Yesterday:

This Week's Goal:

Today's Action Items:

"Think like a queen. A queen is not afraid to fail. Failure is another stepping stone to greatness."
- Oprah Winfrey

Today's Date:

My Affirmation:

Wins From Yesterday:

This Week's Goal:

Today's Action Items:

"I have learned over the years that when one's mind is made up, this diminishes fear; knowing what must be done does away with fear." - Rosa Parks

Today's Date:

My Affirmation:

Wins From Yesterday:

This Week's Goal:

Today's Action Items:

REFLECTIONS

Think of this as your journey's log. Anything you want to take note of so far? This space is great for recording any wins, lessons and ideas for vision expansion.

WEEK 2

I Am Grateful For:
Take a moment to share what you're thankful for.

My Intention For The Week Is:
What magic do you want to create this week?

This Week's Goal:
Reference your goals from your 30 day breakdown.

Action Items To Complete This Week:
Make sure you list the action items from your 30 day breakdown.

"If you're always trying to be normal, you will never know how amazing you can be." - Maya Angelou

Today's Date:

My Affirmation:

Wins From Yesterday:

This Week's Goal:

Today's Action Items:

"There's power in allowing yourself to be known and heard, in owning your unique story, in using your authentic voice." - Michelle Obama

Today's Date:

My Affirmation:

Wins From Yesterday:

This Week's Goal:

Today's Action Items:

"Don't be intimidated by what you don't know. That can be your greatest strength and ensure that you do things differently from everyone else." - Sara Blakely

Today's Date:

My Affirmation:

Wins From Yesterday:

This Week's Goal:

Today's Action Items:

"Let us make our future now, and let us make our dreams tomorrow's reality." - Malala Yousafzai

Today's Date:

My Affirmation:

Wins From Yesterday:

This Week's Goal:

Today's Action Items:

"A woman is the full circle. Within her is the power to create, nurture and transform." - Diane Mariechild

Today's Date:

My Affirmation:

Wins From Yesterday:

This Week's Goal:

Today's Action Items:

"The most common way people give up their power is by thinking they don't have any." - Alice Walker

Today's Date:

My Affirmation:

Wins From Yesterday:

This Week's Goal:

Today's Action Items:

"Giving up doesn't always mean you're weak. Sometimes you're just strong enough to let go." -Taylor Swift

Today's Date:

My Affirmation:

Wins From Yesterday:

This Week's Goal:

Today's Action Items:

REFLECTIONS

Think of this as your journey's log. Anything you want to take note of so far? This space is great for recording any wins, lessons and ideas for vision expansion.

WEEK 3

I Am Grateful For:
Take a moment to share what you're thankful for.

My Intention For The Week Is:
What magic do you want to create this week?

This Week's Goal:
Reference your goals from your 30 day breakdown.

Action Items To Complete This Week:
Make sure you list the action items from your 30 day breakdown.

"I've learned that making a 'living' is not the same as 'making a life.'" - Maya Angelou

Today's Date:

My Affirmation:

Wins From Yesterday:

This Week's Goal:

Today's Action Items:

"It took me quite a long time to develop a voice, and now that I have it, I am not going to be silent."
- Madeleine Albright

Today's Date:

My Affirmation:

Wins From Yesterday:

This Week's Goal:

Today's Action Items:

"You don't have to be pretty. You don't owe prettiness to anyone. Not to your boyfriend/spouse/partner, not to your co-workers, especially not to random men on the street. You don't owe it to your mother, you don't owe it to your children, you don't owe it to civilization in general. Prettiness is not a rent you pay for occupying a space marked 'female.'" -Erin McKean

Today's Date:

My Affirmation:

Wins From Yesterday:

This Week's Goal:

Today's Action Items:

"There's something so special about a woman who dominates in a man's world. It takes a certain grace, strength, intelligence, fearlessness, and the nerve to never take no for an answer." -Rihanna

Today's Date:

My Affirmation:

Wins From Yesterday:

This Week's Goal:

Today's Action Items:

"I love to see a young girl go out and grab the world by the lapels. Life's a bitch. You've got to go out and kick ass." - Maya Angelou

Today's Date:

My Affirmation:

Wins From Yesterday:

This Week's Goal:

Today's Action Items:

"The power you have is to be the best version of yourself you can be, so you can create a better world."
- Ashley Rickards

Today's Date:

My Affirmation:

Wins From Yesterday:

This Week's Goal:

Today's Action Items:

"Doubt is a killer. You just have to know who you are and what you stand for." - Jennifer Lopez

Today's Date:

My Affirmation:

Wins From Yesterday:

This Week's Goal:

Today's Action Items:

REFLECTIONS

Think of this as your journey's log. Anything you want to take note of so far? This space is great for recording any wins, lessons and ideas for vision expansion.

WEEK 4

I Am Grateful For:
Take a moment to share what you're thankful for.

My Intention For The Week Is:
What magic do you want to create this week?

This Week's Goal:
Reference your goals from your 30 day breakdown.

Action Items To Complete This Week:
Make sure you list the action items from your 30 day breakdown.

"Do you want to meet the love of your life? Look in the mirror." - Byron Katie

Today's Date:

My Affirmation:

Wins From Yesterday:

This Week's Goal:

Today's Action Items:

"Buckle up, and know that it's going to be a tremendous amount of work, but embrace it." -Tory Burch

Today's Date:

My Affirmation:

Wins From Yesterday:

This Week's Goal:

Today's Action Items:

"Define success on your own terms, achieve it by your own rules, and build a life you're proud to live."
- Anne Sweeney

Today's Date:

My Affirmation:

Wins From Yesterday:

This Week's Goal:

Today's Action Items:

"We need to accept that we won't always make the right decisions, that we'll screw up royally sometimes – understanding that failure is not the opposite of success, it's part of success." -Arianna Huffington

Today's Date:

My Affirmation:

Wins From Yesterday:

This Week's Goal:

Today's Action Items:

"One of the most courageous things you can do is identify yourself, know who you are, what you believe in and where you want to go." - Sheila Murray Bethel

Today's Date:

My Affirmation:

Wins From Yesterday:

This Week's Goal:

Today's Action Items:

"Everything is within your power, and your power is within you." -Janice Trachtman

Today's Date:

My Affirmation:

Wins From Yesterday:

This Week's Goal:

Today's Action Items:

"Life is not about waiting for the storms to pass. It's about learning how to dance in the rain." -Vivian Greene

Today's Date:

My Affirmation:

Wins From Yesterday:

This Week's Goal:

Today's Action Items:

"Creating the culture of burnout is the opposite of creating a culture of sustainable creativity."
- Arianna Huffington

Today's Date:

My Affirmation:

Wins From Yesterday:

This Week's Goal:

Today's Action Items:

REFLECTIONS ON

For each question below set a timer for 2 minutes. Meditate on each question & write down your answers unedited. Allow your thoughts to flow authentically.

What wins did you have the last 4 weeks?

What graditutdes from the last 4 weeks stand out?

What was accomplished in regards to your big dream?

What lessons did you learn?

THE LAST 4 WEEKS

Anything else you'd like to remember about these past 4 week? New ideas, inspiration, or words of wisdom?

ARE YOU READY TO KEEP PUSHING FORWARD!?

Of course you are!

Keep pushing forward. If you're ready to repeat this system, grab your 90 day planner online. Use the code: *yesunicorn* for 10% off at unicornexchange.com/90

It follows the exact framework that you completed over the last 4 weeks. Each month, you'll get centered on your vision and figure out what your next 3 goals are to move the needle forward on making your dreams a reality.

Once again, I want to take a moment to recognize how much work you've put in to making your dreams come true. When people think of unicorns they think of fluffy, pink creatures nearly synonymous with stuffed toys. That's not true though.

Unicorns are mystical, magical, fierce, and not to be toyed with. They're basically dinosaur horses, for fucks sake. That's what you are. Not to be underestimated or trifled with. Full of magic.

Everything is Possible,

Lauren Andrews
Founder, Unicorn Exchange

MY UNDYING GRATITUDE

I have no idea how I got so fucking lucky. I have so many magical people in my life. For the sake of not creating an entirely separate book on those I owe so much, I limit myself to those that made this possible.

My Unicorn Exchange Underground gang who inspire me every single day: Yelena Reese, Nikki Mocerino, Diana Szczepanska, Stephanie Warner, Abby Miller, Elizabeth Hamilton, CJ Lemky, Brittanie Campbell-Turner, Carrie Silver, Yifat Cohen, Kate Harlow, Rachel Fox, Elissa Williams, Dawna Gonzales, Dijana Llugolli, & Priyanka Khandalkar.

Stephanie Warner, Diana Szczepanska, & Brian Robertson for years of support, laughs, and tears while UE got off the ground. OG crew for life.

Linh Nguyen for being my daily support, magic maker, & making this book (amongst so many things) real. I'm in awe of all you do and how much you teach me.

My forevers: Hannah Wilson for your tireless editing and support. Abby Miller for always adding to my crazy ideas. Kieran Brodie for being my longest, always there stable rock. Nikki Mocerino for reminding me everything is possible. Staci for being the best sister a girl could ask for. Yelena Reese for being my bonus sister and business bestie, none of this would be real without you.

Finally, Frank Mocerino. Thank you for not letting me let my dreams drift away. For late night popcorn while I work like a maniac , my favorite comedian, & my biggest cheerleader. You are my always.

You all are my world and what truly gives me purpose and joy in life. Grateful has and will always be an understatement. Life would be bleak without each and every one of you. Thank you XOXO

www.ingramcontent.com/pod-product-compliance
Lightning Source LLC
Chambersburg PA
CBHW060507030426
42337CB00015B/1780